Amid

Thirsty

Vines

Also by Alfa:

I Find You
in the Darkness

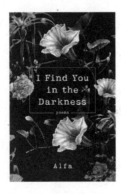

Poems

Amid

Thirsty

Vines

Alfa

Castle Point Books
New York

www.stmartins.com
www.castlepointbooks.com

The Castle Point Books trademark is owned by
Castle Point Publishing, LLC. Castle Point books
are published and distributed by St. Martin's Press.

ISBN 978-1-250-20261-1 (trade paperback)

Our books may be purchased in bulk for promotional,
educational, or business use. Please contact your local
bookseller or the Macmillan Corporate and Premium Sales
Department at 1-800-221-7945, extension 5442, or by email
at MacmillanSpecialMarkets@macmillan.com.

First Edition: October 2018

10 9 8 7 6 5 4 3 2 1

Contents

1
Greenhouse

61
Growing

123
Thriving

Greenhouse

Amid Thirsty Vines

What once was bountiful,
is now barren.
It is always in the wild
and unruly garden
that roots grow deep.
Neglected and forlorn,
resentful buds
and regretful foliage
will wind their way
amid thirsty vines
across a heart's landscape.
If you loved the gardener
enough to let them go,
love yourself enough
to lock the garden gate
after they leave.

Treasure Hunt

You will never
find the depth
of your own soul
by going on
a treasure hunt
in someone else's.

Romp

The weeping willow
swayed back and forth
like a lover shaking her hair
after an afternoon romp.
I could hear the sun's
intake of breath
before he told her
she made beautiful look easy.
—and I was mesmerized
by how his admiration
highlighted her self-confidence.

Growing Naturally

When you find a love that happens as easily
as vines winding around a forgotten tree
stump, you will never have to ask yourself,
"Am I, or am I not?"
And that's the kind of love that will
obliterate doubt and will thrive naturally.

Prison Sentence

What will you do when you realize
that memories have chains
affixed tight across your soul?
Part of you is begging for release,
looking for a pardon that is never coming.
And the other is willing to do *life*
—rather than let go.

Light

Look at how lovely your soul *unfurls*,
as you lean in towards the light.

Fixer

I am a renovator at heart. I see souls who
have potential, and I reach for a
sledgehammer. Every wall that comes down is
a victory for my self-esteem. I wish I could
pass on fixer-uppers and focus on the move-
in ready. But, my vintage soul longs for its
template. I am enamored by the nostalgia,
and character, and the minute and intricate
details that lie hidden beneath the dirt and
grime of a life *trying to live.*

Memory-Laden Mud

My mind likes to imagine. Fantasize a life
where I walk among the hills of flowerbeds
lining pathways, and I never crush their
petals. I create gardens and tend them in
my soul. *Forget-me-nots and daisies,* like
the ones you gave me on our first date.
Planting seedlings and growing flowers
remind me of love, blooming and fragrant.
But then the clouds will ultimately roll in
and water my banks, and more often than
not, it is my tears that flood and overflow
the trenches. And I find myself in the thick
of memory-laden mud, trying to find a way
to climb out.

Pruning

My *heartache* recovery has always entailed pruning my past. It *hurts* to cut out what once made you reach for the sun. But if it is strangling your growth, it must go. And if you are like me, *a hoarder of everything that I once carried,* you will weep enough tears to water the cuttings you tend as you embark on a new season.

Relics

Make no mistake—the agony is stored,
piled high in secret rooms she has no
intention of rearranging or revisiting.
She loads and goes. She hoards their
contents, because even though she refuses
to use them, she is captured by their rarity,
they are collectors to her heart.
She cannot let any of her relics go.

Cashmere

And when all is said and done...
Her spirit may be braced with steel,
but she is cashmere amongst tender skin
and delicate to the touch.

Waiting

My
    heart
will
    wait
for
    you,
even
    if
my
    body
cannot.

Stoic

They're just words, right? Yet when they hit
you with the force of running Clydesdales,
back and forth across your ribcage, you see
how badly spoken words can hurt.
There I stood,
stoic and petrified,
wooden and dust.
Begging this person to love me.
And he said he could not
love my decaying heart.
And that was the end,
but it was also the beginning of *me.*

Revolving Doors

They come and go. A heart can be a
revolving door when it feels empty. I wonder
if we would get an accurate count if we
started counting from the teenage years how
many visitors have come calling. Some stay
longer than others and make rooms in your
heart. You buy matching comforters and
pillow shams and you think this is the one.
The traveling ones only stay for a night.
A traveling heart is never satisfied with
the accommodations and is always looking
for that next *wow* moment. It likes the
adventure, but never gets too comfortable.

Reasons

If he stands at the door, one foot out, bags
already in the car, and asks you to give him
a reason to stay... Gather the strength
you've been holding in tightly. Look him
dead in the eye and give him **100** reasons.
Spill your thoughts and emotions with
explanations so deep that they wash his exit
away. *Because this is it.* The defining line.
Before and after... *him.* You will never get
this moment back. If you don't want him to
go, *he needs to know why.* If you don't
justify his importance in your life, you may
find yourself many years later regretting
never voicing those reasons.
Maybe it was the pent-up anger, or the pride
that held words in your throat, and you
wanted to say it... you wanted to scream,
"Don't go," but you stayed silent. You see,
people leave sometimes, not because they
want to, but because they have no reason
to stay.

Our Kind of Love

I inhale your scent,
pulling you deep within
as familiarity rubs my spine.
My ribs curve,
blinking coquettishly
as your fragrance
strokes the inside
of the place
you call home.

Patience

We end up in relationships
we were never meant
to encounter,
because we were not
patient enough
to wait
for the right one.

Alone

I wonder if we dislike our own company so much that we cling to the ones not meant for us. Anyone who has a warm body and knows how to say *I love you*. We desperately want to believe they speak the truth, because love is all we really want. *Yet we can't find a way to love ourselves.*

Paragraphs

Not every *I love you* requires a paragraph
explanation from your lips.

Pressed Blooms

I leave my imprint
the only way I know how.
A cursive life in bold print.
Answers to questions are often found
in words not spoken,
but coveted like pressed blooms.
Hidden in secret crevices
and scraped from fortified marrow.
I watch as they graft into poetic memories.
I write because I owe these scars
the bedtime story they deserve.

Sediment

We end up planted in relationships we were
not meant to encounter because our bodies
are lonely. We confuse companionship with
comfort. We synchronize closeness with
love. We dig in and try to make the
relationship we find ourselves in... *bloom*.
But if an *authentic love* was not present to
fertilize the union during cultivation,
withering days are ahead.

Tiptoes

She stands on her tiptoes, searching my
eyes for answers.
And all I feel are questions. Things I need
to ask rise in my throat, and I watch her
eyes glide down, seeking solace in my quiet.
And I let it go. And just like that,
a conversation is lost.

Swimming

Here I am
swimming
through the
sea of love,
holding my breath
far too long,
and envious
of those
who stay
on dry land.

Vanilla

I see vanilla-colored roses, but I don't bend
to smell their fragrance, nor do I plant
them among the others I have guarding my
heart's gates.
Because... they remind me of lip balm
kisses at high noon, and candle scents
flickering against bodies in tune.

Holding on

If you're going to hold on,
then hold on so tight
our fingers fuse.
If you're going to keep coming back
every time you go,
then come back and stay.
Put your shoes next to mine,
to the left,
under the stairs
where the space stays vacant.
If you're going to hold on,
then hold on,
and don't ever let go.

Thank you

We don't thank our hearts nearly enough for
all the atrocities we put them through.
We serve them on dinner plates to caveman
souls who don't use napkins and spit them out
because they are well done. We send them into
battle, through horrific experiences, and
expect them to get the job done without
complaining. We object when they are hurting,
and continuously take them for granted
during every minute of our pain. We blame
them for holding on, for having faith when we
have already let go. Yet, they keep tapping
away. Enduring with a strength that is
supernatural *and has nothing to do with us.*
They defy the death sentence you have given
it, and instead keep you and your body alive.
And we don't thank our hearts nearly enough.

Living

When did it hit you?
Turn you inside out,
flip you right where you stood.
When did you feel inspired
to live this life,
instead of merely impaling
your existence?

Reckless

He is reckless abandon,
and she rides on the safe side
of life now.
She knows that the *rush*
is fleeting.
Because nothing *lasting* ever came
from being reckless with her heart.

Before and After

I ask myself... *sometimes when I am alone.*
I ask myself many, many things.
I rarely get the answers to my questions,
but the debates...
the conversations between
who I was *before* you,
and who I am *now*,
are spectacular.

Lyrics

There are songs that can transport you
right back to where it all began. Then there
are others that make you tremble and drop
you where you stand.

Tragedy

People will view your past and call it
a tragedy, *and label you tragic.*
Don't let these words sink in. Remember that
you have endured far worse idle chit-chat
than a few assumptions from naysayers.
Use their judgment as fuel to continue the
bonfire you've already started for *yesterday.*

Runners

There are two kinds of people who walk
away from love.
One is terrified of possessing it
and then losing it, and the other is
altogether numb to it.

Full glass

I'm not looking for the one
who will gallantly tip,
fill me up,
deplete by half,
and then complete me.
The last time I looked,
I was more than a full glass.

Promise me

Promise me that when the roses bloom, the
Winter will have thawed from your heart.
That you will be reminded that a few months
back twigs shivered in uncontrollable
conditions, yet now bud under sunny skies.

Yesterday

Don't waste the magical hours in front of
you trying to fix the minutes you have
already lived. You look back so often,
there is no way you are fully here today.
You must quit living for yesterday.

Inconsistency

I've only known love as fickle as spring
weather. Sunburned on Monday and frozen by
Wednesday. A heart can never plan what it's
going to wear the next day when conditions
are inconsistent.

Heartache

You have to trust in your heart. You have
been bonded since birth. *It depends upon
your caretaking.* It will make undesirable
connections during your lifetime, but you
will need to be understanding during the
hard times. Remember, when *it* hurts . . .
you hurt.

Heart tendrils

Heart connections
are the tendrils
that tangle
against
time,
adversity,
and
intellect.

Bold

Be bold in self-love and self-respect.
Bold enough to waylay the bullies who will
try to take it from you.

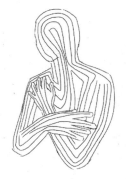

Every Day

I will find you waiting by the fire.
The hearth, where my heart has always been.
My heart has never
left the place
where we were one.
Your hand in mine,
promising to walk
through forest fires.
Finding our way.
Somehow, we got lost.
And I still look for you
e v e r y   d a y.

Dancing

I turned them away, left and right.
The ones who came in place of you.
Willing to fill my emptiness,
and spin me around the dance floor.
But I waited.
I waited because you were the only one
who could make me feel like I was dancing
by merely holding my hand.

Deserving

You are deserving of a love
that captures the photographs
your heart has stored since birth.
You are deserving of a love that finds
the contents of your hope chest
hopeful.

Distraction

Our hearts had a conference.
But we were distracted by our surroundings,
and we never quite focused on the
subject being discussed.

Joy-Riding

I stick my tongue out and feel the cold
glass. I lick the side of the window of my
soul. I feel like a three-year-old child
going on her first vacation. I'm viewing life
differently now. In awe of its wonder and
possibilities. *Thirsty for adventure.*

Perfection

She will not always tell you how she feels
because she has been shushed and shooed
one too many times.
She learned early on that romantic
prospects want perfection, or close to it,
when searching for love. So, she doesn't
reveal much.
She shoveled her concerns into little neat
piles that she hides around the perimeter
of her heart.

Pride Land

There is a place that magically appears
when our integrity is on the line.
We hate to visit, but Pride Land is
always near.

Games

I've never been good at board games of any
kind. I have the kind of heart that takes up
residence in my eyes. One look—and they
always give my next move away, and when you
are transparent, you are easily played.

Fleeting Memory

And when the memories roll in,
causing you to think about him
in a wistful manner.
Eyes of fire that are aflame
when done wrong.
A heart so deep,
the bottom will never
be reached.
Here today,
gone tomorrow.

Howling

The wind is wicked
as it calls to me
under the moonlight.
Perfectly enunciated howls
have turned into:
Your hands are dirty again
from digging through your soul.

Devastation

Storms, I have encountered them in every
season, at every stage in my life.
But he was the only one I named.

Brighter Day

I see the sun peeking through clouds that
have no choice but to part, reminding me
that whatever I face, *there is always hope
for a brighter day.*

Peace

Whenever I ask myself what peace means
to me, I keep coming back to the word
acceptance.
When I finally reached a level of acceptance
within my own heart, I achieved *peace.*
And I will never allow another to take away
what I have spent decades trying to find.

Stout

The cultivating
and the fertilizing
was necessary to grow
stout limbs
and bold petals.
Look at how your center
is highlighted
by the sun.
Even its rays
shine in admiration
at the growth
you have achieved.

Trampled

They cut you off knee-high.
Trampled upon your beauty.
Not knowing that your
loveliness would resurface
another season, and be more
magnificent.

You Will Be Okay

I feel my chest close
and my grip loosen.
I tell them,
and they say
you will be okay.
I forget today
and remember yesterday.
I tell them,
and they say
you will be okay.
I detest being touched
but I need to be felt.
I tell them
and they say
you will be okay.

Stardust

You will not find her in the sea of
your reflection.
She is comprised of things you have never
seen or felt. Stardust clouds her vision
and her heart is tangled in the Moon's glow.
*And it will take light-years to outrun
her memory.*

Lilacs

What is it about the lilacs
and the way they sing your name?
You will always be the scent
that my heart remembers
much too fondly.

Landing

And when my eyes land on you, know that
they see the love you cultivate while
planting kindness for the next generation.

Inspiration

If something is *inspirational*, it should move you to delve deep inside yourself, and help to uncover the hidden gems that pulse with intention and require motivation.

Growing

The Same

We are all going the same way, you know?
On different paths, we meander, breathing
breaths we can never get back. Actions we
have to ask forgiveness for. Realizations
that come too late.
We fill ourselves with the ornamental and
then wonder how they get overgrown. They
overtake our space and smother our chests
if we neglect them. *Every day we plant.*
Sometimes it's words or acts of kindness.
And it might bloom, or the skies will just
carry it away. *But it is never forgotten...*
The Universe saw your intention and
instructed the wind to scatter it somewhere
else far away.

Hands

The hands that hold you
do not own you.
The hands that help you
do not control you.

Who Are You Living For?

It is ingrained in us to want our friends
and family to be proud of us and of the way
we live our live. We say opinions do not
matter, *and they shouldn't,* but we find
ourselves cultivating a common ground.
A neutral place that makes the important
people in our lives content with our life
choices. But when you choose this path,
you are living a life of appeasement,
and your soul will crave authenticity.

Fairytales

You've heard the fairytales. How the man
wrestles the world in order to win the
woman in dire straits.
We grow up groomed by humanity to think
we need saving.
But, let us raise little warriors, who write
their own tales of how they will conquer
the world... and save themselves.

Gazing down

She tiptoes across the Big Dipper
gazing down on the Earth
that she has left behind.
She followed her soul
when it went in search
of home.

Unforgettable

She has transformed
from forgotten,
into *unforgettable*.
And she will not apologize
for living her life with intention.

Future

The unknown days stretched
before her like rubber bands
pulled taut by the Universe.
But she ran toward the future.
Eyes clenched, head down.
Forging onward.
Not daring to look before her.
And always afraid that she would look back.

Saving

One day you will find yourself mesmerized
by eyes much like your own. You will
stare, and recognize the defeat, the level
of despair in which their precious
heart dwells.
You will instinctively reach out, *because
you know*... you know how it feels when your
soul is stifled. When there is absence of
air. *But you pull back*... Because you know
they will have to learn to breathe *their own
air again*. And they cannot do that until
they convince their heart to journey on.
You cannot save everyone. You cannot
browbeat them into *getting over it*.
You can't save everyone—you just can't.
Don't you remember? No one could save
you *from yourself*.

Stand Tall

Stand tall, my love.
You are so much more striking
looking forward,
than looking down.
You do your soul a disservice
by not loving it fully.
Your soul is a spirit being
and it desires love
from the body
in which it dwells.

Old-Fashioned Heart

You have an old-fashioned heart and loving
with every last beat of it does not make you
naïve. It makes you hopeful that you can
make a difference in the lives of those who
have heard the silence too long.

Right Love

His mind and heart
were closed to love,
and it took the *right love*
to convince the
bolted door
to swing wide.

Feast

No matter
how many meals
I have prepared,
the *flavor of us*
is one I can never replicate.

Decisions

Her heart is tumbleweeds and troubled
lands that are subdivided. A landscape
with slopes of yesterday, and a mountainous
range of tomorrows.
She stands uneasy in its epicenter.
Willing herself to turn a blind eye to one,
and to focus on the other.
But one side has him walking amid the
crooks and crannies, and the other is
undiscovered terrain.

Goodbye

I guess I should thank
all the ones
who came before you.
They have allowed
my lips to perfect
saying *goodbye.*
They have taught me
that life *will indeed*
go on.

Good Morning

When they inspire you to crack your shell,
and crawl out—viewing life sunny-side up
instead of scrambled...
Then you know what a good morning
feels like.

Full

We always say *I just want to get
through this*...
I think we foolishly assume that the
Universe dishes out one tribulation per
person. But life is endless dishes with daily
trials. You learn to eat until you're full,
because your heart requires strength to
endure another day.

Autumn Heaven

I have always wondered if heaven captures a time in our lives when we were the happiest and most content. One that mirrored the moment in time when you were in complete and utter love and at peace. And I would like to think that I would spend eternity amid a late-October day with laughter echoing across a long-awaited cool breeze. Crisp ombré leaves will dance in celebration as the rusty gates of my heart open upon candy-corn kisses.

Wild Card

Life will always be the wild card.
You never know what each day will bring,
whether it be storms or a sunny day
so bright, it will burn your blooms.
But just because you have a bad day...
does not mean life is bad.

Too Much

Too much of something beautiful *can hurt.*
Look at how the flowers wilt
when the sun won't leave them alone.

Try to Love You

Just give me more time. I'll be ready to
commit then.
You hear those words and your heart plants
rows of doubt. Because *real* love, *true* love,
is not determined nor managed by a clock.
You either feel it to your toes, or you don't.
Do you think *everlasting, committed-until-*
you-die love is going to suddenly grow from
someone who is sitting on a fence? They
don't even have their feet planted in the
ground, but they expect you to wait a season
and see if love flourishes.
And you know. *You know.*
What this person is saying is they will
try to love you in the way you deserve to
be loved.
Think about this. *Try.*

Learn Her

Learn her. Day by day. There will always be
a new discovery and if you have an
inquiring mind and can convey your
interest in her, *you will learn her.*
She is cinders basking in a glowing fire.
Study abroad in the waves of her
shipwrecked past. You'll find the treasure
trove she has saved for the one she seeks
to spend forever.
Learn her. Become an expert in the language
her heart is fluent in.
Research the volumes of hopeful dreams she
harbors in her soul. Run through her
gardens she has planted with every passion
of her overgrown soul. Pull the ivy from the
walls of her home and make a bonfire out
of her insecurities.
Learn her.

Tears

Tears have a way of making the stone
pillars of her resolve crumble.
They come back, just as she is beginning to
hear the birds sing again. And their pleas
always include heartfelt tears.
And she breaks in pieces, because she wants
to believe that the time apart has brought
him to realizations he did not possess
months ago when he left.
But the tears dry much too soon, and so does
the dust as he leaves again.

Maze

He was hedges
and bad decisions.
Loving him
was always a maze.
And she could never
find her way out.

Begin Again

You are never too old to think about
tomorrow.
Your best days are not past you. If you want
to begin again, *start right now.* A new job,
a new city, a new love.
Every day is a *new beginning.* You can live
as fully at 50 as you did at 30. *You are
never too old to begin again.*
Some life experiences are never meant to be
felt or appreciated until you reach an age
where they are beneficial.

The Hardest Love to Win

And with fate,
came true love.
Eye to eye.
A love fought
with a slayed soul.
With a hollow laugh
and a bended knee.
Self–love is always
the hardest love to win.

Once in a Lifetime

To my once in a lifetime...
Thank you for making me feel the things
I had only read about before holding you.
Thank you for awakening me from slumber
and showing me what I had missed while
choosing to sleep. Thank you for proving
to me that love is more than an emotion
and that it can be a person, a place,
or a memory.

Moving On

I moved on.
I would have waited if you had left me a
light... a small flicker to cut the dark.
But the night grew cold, and my soul crept
towards sunshine. And this new place I have
moved to—is so warm.

Momma's Warning

My mother wanted to protect me, so she
warned me about your kind early on. She
told me you would sweet-talk my novice
heart and tell me what girls want to hear.
My immaturity shook her head and agreed
with everything she said. But even though I
listened *time after time*, I was still drawn
to what I knew meant me harm.

Bookmark

He was my
most used
bookmark.
Always
highlighting
the chapters
we
loved
in.

Surface

If you settle
for surface love,
you will never reap
the kind that grows
root deep.

Missing Out

If you choose to keep your heart hidden by
living a life of quiet and routine, you will
miss out on the kind of chaos that makes
your soul see stars.

Tending Your Own Garden

And when I began to tend *my own garden*,
and raked through my toxic compost pile of
thoughts, my blooms respected their resting
place, and flourished amid the soil in which
they were planted.

Leaving

Be careful how you leave people.
The way you do so will forever
be engraved in their hearts.
And after your exit, they will
always be fearful of doors,
wondering if every time they shut...
it is forever.

Mirrors

We need to spend less time looking
into mirrors and instead gaze deeply
into hearts.
That's where beauty resides, anyway.

Voices

When you are sitting alone
in the quiet,
with nothing to hold on to
except for the way
you feel about yourself...
I hope you do not listen to the *voices*
of those who have left.

Because He Left

When the one you thought was your forever
decides to leave, and you rid yourself of the
aftermath of his toxicity, you will find you
can fill the crevices with things that would
not fit before. The tears were cleansing and
washed away the sands of dismissal. Now
your heart is filled with bountiful fruit
trees. And you grow sweetness, *and you give
it away.* Your rows of herbs are fragrant,
and you accept the healing as you inhale
and exhale the past. You weed daily, lest
the ivy invades your oasis. *And you feel
happiness budding...* and you find that the
world is indeed a beautiful and exciting
place again.
And it happened because he left, *and you had
room to plant a garden.*

Ashes

Say goodbye to the seasons that left you
clinging to the dark. Burn your sentiments
with the saplings you saved from the house
you never got to build. Watch as the evening
wind carries the ashes away.

Letters

Late-night letters that I will never send sit
in stacks under an armoire that plays an
admirable role as my secret accomplice.
I write treasonous words that my heart
dictates via heartbeats when the words
swirling become too much. My mind is a
merry-go-round, and if I do not jump off and
spill the conversations that have *never
been said,* the ones that circle like echoes,
I will surely go mad. I write the letters and
I scribe them eloquently; I even address
them to recipients of my past. The
interlopers. The ones who came, dented my
future, and walked. Pulse after pulse my pen
screams, but it is worth the headache,
because my frustrations ease as I sign
my name.
My voice will stay silent, *like it always has,*
but I am thankful for this form of expression
because it keeps my exterior sane.

Connected

We walk among a crowd of nameless faces day
in, and day out. We're all connected, but we
don't act like we are. Strangers swimming
in and out of the same waters, yet closer
than what we want to believe.

Spring is Coming

Your leaves are falling, and you feel their
loss, but I promise you that you will bud
again. Those branches that have been heavy-
laden need rest and recovery, *because
spring is coming*. You will feel life begin to
ebb again as a ray of sunshine dapples to
your roots, and happiness grafts along the
rings of your inner core.

Tortured

Maybe you are drawn to tortured souls
because you know how it feels to want to
live yet pray to die.

Individuality

Stand tall. Straighten your stem, because
the opinions of others will take their toll.
They will wind themselves around you and
try to choke out your uniqueness. Find your
underpinning and latch on ... and let your
individuality shine. Never change yourself
or shield your authenticity because someone
points out that you are different.

Promises

A bouquet can never make up
for the single rose that was wanted.
And an excuse can never make up
for a promise not kept.

Soul Cleansing

I wonder if a heart will ever give up and
stop remembering, or will memories become
stains that no amount of soul cleansing can
wash away?

Sentimental

Their essence may be embedded in your psyche, but with skill, you will learn how to compartmentalize. You will become an expert at putting them away in dusty bins that you store Christmas decorations in. And with each holiday, you will likely have to endure taking them out and reminiscing over each one. Within those moments nostalgia will lick its lips and make you feel sentimental over history. But you will pack them away, *and you will get through the day.*

Happy

The hardest part of a breakup is watching them make it work with someone else, *and you can do nothing about it*... because you love them enough to want to see them happy. *And they are.*

Shovel

When you weed your soul,
don't forget to get into the cracks
and shovel, or you may find
unwanted dandelions,
rooting and flourishing
seasons later.

Growing Flowers

Your mind will grow beautiful
flowers tomorrow.
But their display depends upon what
you choose to prune back today.

Where I've Been

I carry the hurt of others in my bones.
I work hard to release the pain by trying to
offer a helping hand to those who *are where
I've been.*
And this is how I heal.

Quilting

If you veer from the passions
and the talents
that are sewn
inside the rooms
of your heart,
you will never
quilt a life
that feels like home.

Gathering

They will see your broken pieces, and with
helpful hands will start gathering. Even
though they seem well-meaning, they will try
to reassemble you into their style.
And you will find that the reconfiguration
isn't a perfect fit. Your soul will feel like
it's staying in a hotel and not its home.
And this is why you must never let another
person fix you into a version of their
desires. *You will lose yourself that way.*

Show Them

Use the pain you have held in *to help*
someone else learn to breathe again.
They hurt, and they think they are alone.
Show them how to inhale and exhale.
Show them how you breathe in today...
and exhale yesterday.

Rose

A heart responds like a rose.
Closed and captivating,
until sunshine steps in.
And then watch it unfold.
One by one
petals unbind,
and bask in the warmth
of adoration
it has never
known before.

Tangled

I always find you
tangled in my senses,
wrapped around
my fences.

Secret Garden

Just because someone enters your life does
not mean they have an all-access pass to
your soul. You are not required to allow
visitors to take a tour through the
manicured and carefully cultivated
pathways of your secret garden.

Sprouting

When you give yourself time to heal after
heartache, you will feel flowers pushing
forth from openings that you thought would
never close. And you will wear your
newfound beauty with a grace to be envied.

Teach Them

I hear them say that loving oneself is
narcissism. And I could not *disagree* more.
Of course, if you love yourself, *and only
yourself,* that is a narcissistic demeanor.
But, a measure of self-love is necessary to
keep your heart from being mauled by a
narcissistic society.
Having love for your own heart and soul
enables you to love others on a deeper and
more empathetic level. Love yourself enough
to set an example for children that love is
not an emotion to be earned but is
unconditional and to be given freely.
How can you exude a kind heart and profess
to give love unselfishly to others when you
do not apply the same principle to your own
spirit? Saying you don't like yourself but
love others does not make you a martyr or
admirable... it makes you look cold and
dead. You will exhibit a robot going through
the motions with hands that do anything for
public show.
Teach others that a measure of love begins
within, as young as possible. And maybe,
just maybe, they will not spend the rest of
their lives jumping from soul to soul,
trying to find the universe that already
lives inside them.

Change

I feel myself changing. Even a landscape
can change after 20 years. You will revisit
a place from your past and not recognize a
single landmark.
But if you look closely, you will find your
initials carved on the big oak at the foot of
your heart. And you will sit on a slatted
bench and you will reminisce about long
ago. But, you will get homesick. And if you
are honest with yourself, you know that home
now feels better than 20 years ago.

Take Something Away

Take something away from every interaction
you encounter. Good or bad, you can learn
from it. Admire it. Detest it. But don't
regret it. Never regret anything that taught
you a valuable life lesson.

Forgiving Heart

I forgave myself
after I forgave you.
And this is how
I accepted the apology
you never gave me.

Carnival

She felt ancient, not in years but in
experience. She looks left, then right, and
she sees amusement park eyes and the circus
hearts of today's *single and available*.
Dating has turned into a freak show, and
she is thinking *she is the freak.* The cotton
candy and the boardwalk games going on
around her hold no temptation. She hears
noise that is meant to be jovial and she
wants no part of the carnival rousing
through the quiet her mind craves.

Thriving

Shut

I didn't want to wake you as I saw that you were finally sleeping after nine days of barely any. I know this is hard on you, and I'm sorry.
P.S. I promise to keep my mouth shut next time...
—Your Heart

Fitting In

You may feel like you don't fit in or you do
not belong. But in my eyes, *you stand out.
And your beauty is incandescent.*

Imprint

Their imprint you try so hard to forget will never completely dissolve. The residue will always linger. *In time* it will become opaque, and they will loosen their leash on your heart, and you will be clear to live *in this moment.*

Sacred Place

I allowed you into a sacred place.
The corner of my world where hydrangeas
decorate skin like jewelry. Where candy-tuft
and phlox mound to lay your weary head.
You explored the flower gardens with
curious steps and remarked upon the rarity
of the plantings. I welcomed you into my
sacred place *and shared with you the
backyard of my soul.*

Savage

When you are connected to a person, you feel
their pain and its savage teeth grinding
back and forth. You remember it's not *your*
physical hurt to bear, but your heart is
invested, and wants to provide healing...
anything to make the gnashing go away.

Fertilizer

When a soul cries it releases the fertilizer
that is needed to ready the landscape for
new beginnings.

Caretaker

If you do not assume
the role as caretaker
of your own heart,
someone
else
will.

Anything

You can dress up
practically anything
and make it
look good.
Anything.
But if a heart
is ugly,
no amount
of makeup,
high heels,
or camera filters
can make
it lovely.

Full Belly

He hurt you and swallowed your dreams
whole. And somewhere out there he is still
strutting around with a full belly and an
even bigger appetite. Carnivores never
change their diet.

Old Thoughts

I know it is hard to believe but those
thoughts you have running through your
mind will find their way out one day. And
little by little new ones will creep in like
ivy, and wind around your heart, replacing
your yesterday with today.

Reborn

You have always wondered why you feel
things to your core. Experiencing feelings
that shake you and turn your bones to dust.
And it is because you are blessed and cursed
with an empathetic heart that sees the
revival in destruction. You have witnessed
beauty emerging from the burial grounds of
your past, and you know how it feels to die
and to be reborn.

Not Broken

Just because it differs than what we are
accustomed to, *we try to fix what is
not broken.*
We ache to transform, mold, and shape
another, so they fit into our idea of *normal.*
In some warped sense of justification, we
think we love someone so much that we need
to fix them.
But, true love is not about fixing someone.
True love is about accepting someone and
all their unique intricacies.
True love is *absolute and infinite*
acceptance.

Purpose

We know how powerful memories are.
You would think we would live purposely to
create ones that are a joy to entertain.

Departure

I have been tested many times in this life,
and my strength has grown throughout every
episode. But if I had to pinpoint a time when
I didn't think I'd survive, it was when my
level of endurance was tested while
watching the flowers grow on the sands of
your departure.

Do Not Ignore It

You are told to heal, and you promise
yourself you will take the time. But healing
cannot happen by ignoring the heart and
soul that is still writhing in pain. The
neglect will cause the healing to come to a
halt. *Tend to the pain.* Nurture your heart
as it has a good cry. Wrap it up in a blanket
and rock it to sleep while telling it a
bedtime story if you have to. *But, do not
ignore it.* Acknowledge the hurt, and from
there you can get through it, *together.*

True Love

If it is true love, the only thing that can
separate you from that love is death.
And even then, you will wait patiently until
it is your time to join them once again.

Battles

Once he realized
that she was more
than capable
of handling
her own
battles,
he put
his armor down
and took
her hand.

The Right Way

How many times do we walk away because
someone did not say *I love you* in the
right way?

Shade of Forever

He knew he loved her before he ever saw her
eye color, because her heart was the perfect
shade of forever.

One

My
heart
used
to
beat
for
one.
Before him.

Crush

We say one thing, *but we feel another.* We say we are okay, when we are anything but. We do this to make ourselves hold on to the hope that *we will be okay,* someday. Because when someone crushes the foliage of your soul, you have no choice but to use it as mulch for a new season of growth.

Quest for Love

And at the end of the day, we will do anything to find love *but are clueless at keeping it.*

Residency

Why is it
we always assume
that our hopes,
dreams,
and passions
reside within
another heart?

Arbors

I have built arbors to hold the trailing
vines of my past. I let them decorate the
boundaries of my garden so that anyone who
comes to visit will see what I have come
from, *and how I have grown into the person I
am today.*

Unsettling

There are those who find storms unsettling,
and then there are others who *find the calm*
in the midst of a raging downpour.

Us

Every once in a while, my soul will fold upon
itself as I read *the last chapter of us.*

The Ones

I adore the ones that have a petal bent, or a leaf mottled from too much sun. The ones that have freckles because the bugs loved them too much. The ones that stand just as tall as their neighbors who look *untouched*. I love the ones who show that their existence has mattered. That they have fought off the birds who like to pick, and the animals who like to burrow. I love the ones who do not shirk and still turn their sunny faces toward the sky, standing tall until their stem bends and their last bloom is carried away.
I love how they seed the land to rise again another day.

Rebellion

She blooms with rebellion, like wild
honeysuckle winding through a ranch's
fence. And every time she rolls across your
fingers, her scent of freedom will waft
without a trace of remorse.

Love is Not a Well

Love does not run out. It is never-ending.
Give every last drop to the person you love,
and before you can blink, it will be
replenished.
Never say you gave all your love away.
You have reserves you've never even tapped
into. Love is not a well. It can't dry up.
It's there... flowing through your veins.
Always ready to pour out.

Searching

She did not need anyone to battle *for her*.
But she thought of someone battling the
Universe *to find her*, and that appealed
to her.

Words

Words upon lips
will always be
my downfall.
How I ache
to be read to,
watching lips part
and literature spill.

Recovery

Recovery happens day by day, and you will have setbacks along the way. Life happens, and stress makes you revert to old habits. You will feel momentarily empty, and for a time you will think of turning around, one step in the wrong direction—*yesterday*. But you are stronger now, and it has become easier to say no. It has taken a lot of struggles to get you to today. And you will not trade today *for any amount of yesterday*.

Ultimatum

The truth is you never know the depth of the strength you possess, or how you will choose to wield it until life busts through your front door with an ultimatum.

About Them

If it is always about *them*,
remove yourself.
And don't insert yourself again.

Darkness Calls

He holds her hand at night, not because
she is fearful of the darkness, but because
he knows she once called it home. And he
holds on tight because he does not want her
to return.

Warning

If it is easy, neat, and sectioned;
structured, normal, and runs like clockwork;
chances are we will not like it. Not for
long, anyway. We say we want all that, and
eventually we will settle for a version of it,
but our hearts are always drawn to the ones
who came and left without warning.

Holding Doors

I have held the door open wide,
letting love in.
It dove in and plowed through.
I fed it.
And basked in it.
Gave it room and board.
I have held the door open wide,
and watched it leave.

Generations

When we look back—*because we all will*—
I hope we can say that we planted love in
hearts that grew tall and wide and lived on
to tell stories to future generations.

Pit Stop

All those stops along the way ultimately
lead you to a destination. Some stops were
just gas stations that we mistook for places
to build a home. We got confused because our
hearts ran out of gas, and we think when
that happens that we should stay wherever
we land and grow. *But if you are just
existing and not flourishing,* you need to
fill up—and go.

Posies

You will glance down and notice clusters of posies at your feet, and you will touch their tenderness, rubbing your hand back and forth, tempted to pick some to take home. But you know how it feels to be plucked and put on display until you wither away.
So, you leave the mound intact, because you will not remove it from the environment in which it thrives.

Magicians

A person's true intentions will always be
revealed. Even a magician shares his
secrets after a certain amount of time
has passed.

Facing Problems

If you are always running from problems,
you will never find the answers that you
seek. Face each one head on. Deal with it
and move on. But never let something minute
branch into bushes that you will have to
remove later on.

Roaming Free

Orchids may be revered for their elegance and beauty, but they are envious of the wildflowers who get to roam free.

Intimidation

They view you as hard and strong, and that
terrifies people who are less self-confident.
They will never understand the necessity
behind the erection of your protection.
What they view as *hardness* is in fact
protection from the ones who feasted off
your softness in the past.
The people who walk away from you now
because they are intimidated by your
strength and find it unappetizing are the
same kind who ate freely while thinking
you *weak.*

Brilliant Display

New stems have grafted
onto the branches of my heart
that used to connect to you.
The very thing that you broke free
of has blossomed into a bouquet
of brilliance that fills
someone else's garden.
And I just wanted to say,
thank you.

Climbing Terrains

I have climbed rocky terrains, trying to
outrun the cutting remarks of those who
look me right in the face with a smile,
masking the knife in their mouth.

Outrunning a Memory

If we teach them to run fast
at the first sight of disrespect,
then they won't have to
waste precious years
outrunning their memory.

Negative Space

I found out the hard way that if you fill
your freshly emptied heart with negative
space, it will sow prickly thoughts that
torture you with slanderous accusations.
Plant some marigolds instead.
They never hurt a soul.

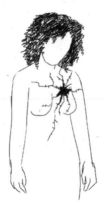

Humming

When I find the weight of the world becoming
too heavy to bear, I find a place where I can
shut out the noise and start *humming*. I hum
to silence the traffic, the doorbell, and
the sirens. Anything that causes my heart
to race. I hum to silence my soul from its
inquisition. I hum to soothe my heart
to sleep.

Dreamcatcher

I placed a dreamcatcher in the garden of my soul tonight. My wish is that I will somehow capture the hopes and dreams of the seedlings I have planted—*and ensure a bountiful harvest.*

Full Moon

You must be careful when meeting love under the magic of a full moon. It even makes a cemetery *vibrate with life* and feel everlasting when cast under its deceptive glow.

Get Through It

When you feel small and unseen, and ill
equipped to handle life's insurmountable
obstacles, take a moment to sit. Shut your
eyes and inhale the silence. Listen to your
heart beating. It's reassuring you that it is
with you all the way. Don't forget to exhale.
Never let quitting cross your mind. You have
come too far for that. Reevaluate. Ask for
help if you can and readjust your plan.
There is always a way to *get through it.*

Cottonmouth

Raindrops
have
supernatural
powers
and
quench
the
cottonmouth
of
a
heart
that
has
been
thirsty
too
long.

Sucker Punch

Unconditional love does not flinch when life
gives it a sucker punch.

Heart and Soul

A heart and a soul are two distinctly
different entities.
They have discussions back and forth, always
debating as to who is the boss *of you*.
The heart likes to remind your soul that it
is vital because it keeps the body alive by
pumping its blood and without it you would
surely die.
And the soul always counters back, "Imagine
that. I'm alive and I don't even need a
heart."

Don't Hover

If you give them just enough space, *void of your shadow*, they can lie under the stars and see the magical lightshow with you.

Walking Upright

I think sometimes we get so comfortable
kneeling and bending over. We have become
so complacent in tending the soil of our
lands and praying for bountiful harvests,
that this position has become almost
normalcy.
We forget that we were meant to walk *upright
on this earth.*

Ping Pong

Challenge me.
Make me think.
It's been a long time since anyone has
sparked a fire within my frozen stairwells.
Pique my interest. Make my curiosity ask for
more. Let's talk about the weather, or the
desert, or race cars. Tell me something that
will make my pulse race and my mind
process. I have been numb to conversation
for so long that I crave the banter that is
served back and forth between equally
matched players in a game of ping pong.

Time

I have checked my watch a thousand times
and knowing it has been four years' worth
of 24-hour days since I saw you last does
not make it easier. *With, or without time.*

Happy Tears

He told me I had so much to give, but I could
never quite understand what he meant by it.
He told me I could not see it because it
resided within me and that one day I would
find it. I didn't understand how he could
see it if I stared in the mirror every day
and never saw anything but a sad state of
affairs. The more time I spent with him I
felt myself smiling. Little smiles here and
there would overtake me, and he would catch
me and say *do that again.* And of course
I could not. But then it happened. I found
myself smiling one day at his silly antics
and I broke out into a full-blown belly
laugh. He stood there slack-jawed. He told me
to *run to the mirror and see if I noticed
anything different.* I looked at myself in
the mirror and I could not believe how
happy and refreshed and how revived
I looked.

He came up behind me, holding me close and
told *me that this was the first time he had
ever seen me cry happy tears, as he had only
seen my cry painful ones.* And then I looked
up and he had tears in his eyes too. And he
said *Don't worry, these are most definitely
happy tears.*

Sated

And when he proclaimed to love me,
he accepted the unsavory
along with the sustenance.
And I have never
let him go hungry
a day since.

Should you ever find yourself

standing before a mirror of self-loathing and indescribable loss, asking yourself *if you can get through it*... Wondering how you will ever begin again amongst the raided and barren land that he has left in his wake. *You are not alone.*

You must begin right now and right where you are. You gather what is left and you embrace a new season. The land may be stripped away but you can sow new seed. Unearth the toxicity and cultivate a garden in your soul.

You are thinking you will never find love again, *but you will*. And you do not want to attract the same kind as before. This is why it is so important that you take care of your heart and your soul and prepare them for the *right kind of love* that you are deserving of.

And I promise you when your heart is ready to embark again, you will find yourself wrapped in a love that is worthy of you... *amid thirsty vines.*

About the Poet

Alfa would paint the world in hues of turquoise if she could. Unapologetic about her realistic take on heartache, she writes to let her readers know they are not alone in their pain. Her four children and three granddaughters, the stars of her life, were the catalysts that pushed her to force her words and her smile on the world after a lifetime of depression and anxiety. She wanted to leave something behind for them, a legacy, proof of existence, and proof that pain can be transformed into beautiful inspiration. Alfa lives in Louisville, Kentucky.